REFLECTIVE EXERCISE BOOK (KEYPOINTS) FOR JON FAVREAU'S DEMOCRACY OR ELSE

ISBN :
written by:
year of publication: 2024

THIS BOOK BELONGS TO:

Table of Contents

Introduction: The Urgency of Now

Few moments in the vast tapestry of history have the seismic power to completely alter a country. We are standing on the brink of such a moment right now, one that could decide the future of American democracy. The book "Democracy or Else: How to Save America in 10 Easy Ways," written by Jon Favreau, Jon Lovett, Tommy Vietor, and Josh Holloway, serves as a manual and a wake-up call for the public, imploring them to see the potential dangers to our democracy and take prompt action to protect it.

One cannot stress how urgent this moment is. The United States, which has long been hailed as a model of democracy, is currently dealing with a number of issues that threaten the foundation of its system of government. Numerous forces are working to undermine the fundamental values of the rule of law, vibrant civic involvement, and free and fair elections. The obstacles are severe but not insurmountable, ranging from systematic voter suppression and the corrupting power of large money in politics to the spread of false information and widening social divides.

This introduction lays the groundwork for a thorough investigation into ways to strengthen and revitalize American democracy. It is a rallying cry for everyone who values the liberties and obligations that come with being a member of a democratic society. It is an appeal to acknowledge that maintaining democracy is a shared task that necessitates the active involvement of every person rather than the exclusive province of activists or elected officials.

The Decline of Faith and the Ascent of Skepticism

The rate at which people's trust in democratic institutions has been eroding is concerning. A sizeable segment of the public displays skepticism regarding the fairness of elections, the independence of the courts, and the effectiveness of legislative bodies. The constant onslaught of false information and misinformation, which is frequently spread via social media sites that value sensationalism over reality, feeds this distrust. As a result, the electorate becomes more and more divided into echo chambers where agreement and compromise become harder to come by.

Democracy is seriously threatened by the current surge of cynicism. Authoritarian inclinations can emerge when people lose faith in the institutions that serve them, leading to disengagement and disillusionment. The deterioration of democratic standards gives individuals more confidence to subvert the system for their own or their party's benefit. We need to recommit to the principles of accountability, truth, and transparency in order to buck this trend. The ensuing chapters provide specific actions to accomplish these objectives, ranging from defending the right to vote to battling false information.

The Need for Civic Involvement

A thriving democracy depends on its people taking an active role in it. Nonetheless, there has been a downturn in civic involvement in the US, with voter turnout falling short of that of other industrialized countries and civic education getting little focus in school curricula. People who do not care about the public interest can take advantage of the void left by this disengagement.

This trend needs to be reversed with a diversified strategy. To equip the next generation with the information and abilities needed to actively participate in democratic processes, we must invest in civic education. In order to encourage residents to participate in community organizing, attend town hall meetings, and keep their legislators responsible, we also need to establish channels for public participation outside of the voting booth. The tactics presented in this book are intended to promote an atmosphere of engaged citizenship, in which each person understands that their actions have an impact on the destiny of their democracy.

Addressing Systemic Disparities

The promise of justice and equality for all people is at the core of the democratic ideal. However, structural injustices still afflict American society, eroding the credibility of democratic institutions and stoking animosity among the downtrodden. Gender inequality, economic inequality, and racial discrimination are democratic problems that demand immediate response; they are not just social problems.

Not only is it morally required to address these disparities, but it is also practically necessary for democracy to survive. Policies that are inclusive and advance social justice, economic equity, and equal opportunity can help rebuild trust in the system and create a feeling of common purpose. This book explores the underlying causes of these disparities and offers doable fixes to build a society that is more just and equal.

The Significance of Collective Action and Leadership

Navigating the intricacies of democratic governance requires effective leadership. True transformation, however, necessitates grassroots collaboration in addition to top-down leadership. Significant democratic advances throughout history have been fueled by the coordinated efforts of common people who refused to accept the status quo.

This book emphasizes how cooperation and unity may propel democratic improvements. It gives readers helpful advice on how to begin or join their own initiatives and movements, and it presents instances of movements and activities that have been effective in bringing about significant change. Together, we can make a powerful force for change by raising the volume of our voices.

A Renewal Road Map

"Democracy or Else: How to Save America in 10 Easy Ways" offers a road map for revitalization as well as a critique of the status quo. Every chapter provides a thorough analysis of a particular facet of democracy, such as defending voting rights, regulating political contributions, encouraging public participation, and squelching false information. The answers put out are realistic, doable actions that can actually make a difference rather than lofty ideals.

This book is proof of the democracy's tenacity and the enduring strength of the American spirit. For everyone who thinks that a government of the people, by the people, and for the people is possible, it is a call to action. We must act immediately to protect the democratic values that guide our country and to make sure that the democracy that comes to be in the future is more robust and inclusive than it has ever been.

As you begin your journey through the pages of "Democracy or Else," we encourage you to consider your part in this crucial time. Democracy is a participatory undertaking that demands the dedication and engagement of every person; it is not a spectator sport. By working together, we can overcome the obstacles in our way and create a better future for everybody. It is time to take action.

Chapter 1: Protecting Voting Rights Ensuring Access for All Introduction: The Foundation of Democracy

Democracy is built on the foundation of voting rights. Voting gives people a voice in their government and helps to hold elected officials responsible. However, throughout American history, the freedom to vote has consistently been threatened, despite its essential significance. Disenfranchised populations have been denied the right to vote by a variety of strategies, including literacy tests, poll taxes, voter ID legislation, and purges of the voter rolls.

This chapter will look at the evolution of voting rights in the US, the problems that voters face today, and practical solutions to make sure that all eligible citizens may exercise their right to vote.

A Synopsis of American Voting Rights History

In America, the struggle for the right to vote has been protracted and difficult. Voting was initially restricted to white male property owners. Over time, a number of campaigns and laws were passed to increase voting rights:

1. Although African American men were given the right to vote by the 15th Amendment (1870), systemic racism and discriminatory practices such as Jim Crow laws severely restricted their ability to exercise that privilege.
2. The 19th Amendment (1920): This important win for the women's suffrage campaign gave women the right to vote.
3. Racial discrimination in voting was addressed by the Voting Rights Act of

1965, which was especially prevalent in the South. This historic statute prohibited literacy tests and other forms of discrimination, and it mandated that areas with a track record of discrimination obtain federal clearance before making changes to their voting rules (a clause that was somewhat undermined by the 2013 Shelby County v. Holder ruling by the Supreme Court).
4. The 26th Amendment (1971) lowered the voting age from 21 to 18 in recognition of younger people's maturity and sense of civic duty, especially in light of the Vietnam War.

The Current Threats to Voting Rights

Notwithstanding these developments, other obstacles to voting have surfaced recently. Among them are:

1. Voter ID laws: While supporters claim that these laws stop fraud, in reality, they disproportionately impact low-income, elderly, and minority voters who might not have the necessary documentation.
2. Voter Roll Purges: States take inactive voters off their lists on a regular basis. Even though the goal is to keep correct records, this might lead to the erroneous removal of qualified voters—often without their awareness.
3. Closing of Polling stations: Fewer polling stations lead to long queues and make voting more challenging, especially in rural and minority populations.
4. Gerrymandering: When election district lines are drawn to give one party preference over another, the idea of equal representation is compromised.
5. Felon Disenfranchisement: A lot of states deny voting rights to people who have served their sentences for felonies, which disproportionately affects African American communities.
6. Misinformation: Voters may become disoriented and discouraged if intentionally misleading information concerning voting procedures is disseminated.

Providing Access for All: Approaches and Remedies

Ensuring universal access and safeguarding voting rights require fundamental reforms. The following are important tactics:

1. National Law to Preserve Voting Rights

Restore the Voting Rights Act: By eliminating the need for some states to seek federal consent before making changes to their voting laws, the Supreme Court's ruling in Shelby County v. Holder severely undermined the Voting Rights Act. For these safeguards to be strengthened and restored, new legislation must be passed by Congress.

a. Pass the For the People Act, a comprehensive bill that addresses campaign money corruption and gerrymandering while providing opportunities for same-day and automatic voter registration.

c. The John Lewis Voting Rights Advancement Act: This law, which bears the late civil rights activist's name, attempts to bring back the Voting Rights Act's complete protections and guarantee that any modifications to voting regulations be carefully considered for any possibility of discrimination.

Reforms at the State Level

a. Automatic Voter Registration (AVR): Unless they want to opt out, states should implement AVR, which registers eligible citizens to vote whenever they deal with government entities (such as when obtaining a driver's license).

a. Same-Day Registration: Encouraging voters to register and cast their ballots on the same day not only boosts turnout but also makes sure that eligible voters aren't prevented from doing so by last-minute registration problems.

c. No-Excuse Absentee and Early Voting: By offering these choices, it makes sure that voters who face obstacles such as schedule problems or medical conditions can still cast ballots.

d. Restore Voting Rights for Former Felons: States ought to automatically reinstate former felons who have served out their sentences and are reintegrating into society by granting them the ability to vote.

a. Prevent gerrymandering by forming impartial redistricting commissions to create equitable electoral district lines and guarantee that each and every vote is treated equally.

3. Increasing Accessibility to Polling Places

a. Expand the Number of Polling Locations: Make sure that polling stations are easily accessible to all voters, especially in underprivileged areas.

a. Extend Polling Hours: Extended hours, such as options for early morning and late evening, help voters who have other obligations or irregular work schedules.

c. Provide Transportation Assistance: Particularly in rural and low-income regions, provide transportation choices for voters who do not have dependable access to polling places.

4. Outreach and Education Programs

a. Voter Education Campaigns: Start extensive campaigns to enlighten the public on election dates, registration requirements, and their rights to vote. To reach a large audience, use a variety of channels, such as social media.

a. Civic Education in Schools: To teach young people the value of voting and how to take part in the electoral process, schools should implement comprehensive civic education programs.

c. Community Outreach: To engage and mobilize voters, especially in historically marginalized communities, collaborate with local leaders, church organizations, and community organizations.

5. Eliminating False Information
a. Fact-Checking Resources: Make readily available hotlines and fact-checking resources available to voters so they can counter false information and confirm details about voting procedures.

a. Media Literacy Initiatives: Establish initiatives to instruct people in the critical assessment of information sources and the identification of inaccurate or misleading material.

c. Social Media Monitoring: Collaborate with social media sites to swiftly detect and eliminate misleading information about elections and voting.

Case Studies: Effective Voting Rights Proposals

Analyzing successful campaigns can yield insightful information about practical methods for preserving voting rights:

1. Oregon's Automatic Voter Registration (AVR): In 2016, Oregon became the first state to adopt AVR. Voter registration rates have risen dramatically since then, especially for young and minority voters.

2. Florida's Amendment 4: Voters in Florida approved Amendment 4 in 2018, restoring the majority of those with felony convictions who had served out their terms to the ability to vote. This resulted in the restoration of voting

rights for about 1.4 million Floridians.

3. Early Voting in North Carolina: The state's decision to extend early voting has boosted voter participation, especially among African Americans, who had previously encountered considerable obstacles on election day.

The Function of Grassroots Movements and Advocacy

Protection and expansion of voting rights are largely dependent on advocacy and grassroots movements. In order to combat discriminatory practices and advance voter access, groups like the ACLU, NAACP Legal Defense Fund, and the League of Women Voters have been at the forefront of this battle, utilizing advocacy, public education, and litigation.

Community organizing is powerful, as seen by the efforts of grassroots groups like those headed by Stacey Abrams in Georgia. By registering hundreds of thousands of voters and opposing voting suppression strategies, Abrams's Fair Fight Action initiatives have helped lead to historic voter turnout and election triumphs.

Conclusion: The Way Ahead

Maintaining voting rights is about more than just making sure that people can cast ballots; it's about defending democracy itself. Voting gives every citizen a say in how our nation is run, and democracy is undermined when that voice is suppressed or ignored.

We may move in the direction of a more equal and inclusive electoral system by putting the tactics discussed in this chapter into practice. Reforms at the federal and state levels, enhanced accessibility for polling places, instructional programs, and dispelling false information are all essential elements of this endeavor.

Still, these steps are insufficient on their own. To protect the right to vote and guarantee that every American may fully engage in our democracy, it takes a consistent commitment from all of us—citizens, activists, legislators, and community leaders.

As we proceed, let us never forget that our democracy is strongest when it is inclusive and easily accessible. We pay tribute to the people who gave their lives defending voting rights and lay the foundation for a more equitable and democratic society by defending and extending these rights.

We must act now because of the urgency. Let's take up the challenge and band together to defend the voting rights that are the foundation of our democracy.

CHAPTER 2: Reforming Campaign Finance
- Ending Big Money's Influence

When large money controls the political process, the integrity of democratic governance is put at risk. This chapter explores the background and implications of campaign finance rules, with a special emphasis on the Citizens United v. FEC ruling from the Supreme Court, which legalized unlimited corporate spending in elections. The political landscape has been distorted by the flood of cash from dark money organizations and super PACs, which has given affluent donors and special interests excessive influence.

The necessity to reverse Citizens United is the first step in the chapter's exploration of several strategies for campaign finance reform. The article talks about how public financing can help level the playing field for politicians and the possibility of a constitutional change to restrict campaign expenditures. Examples of effective public finance systems enacted in places like Maine and Arizona show the viability and advantages of such reforms.

Transparency is yet another important component. In order to ensure that voters are aware of who is supporting political campaigns and influencing their elected leaders, the chapter pushes for strict disclosure laws on political spending and donations. It also emphasizes how important it is to have strong enforcement procedures in place in order to stop corruption and punish offenders.

The chapter illustrates how lessening the impact of money in politics might result in more responsive and equitable governance through case studies and In order to advance social justice, economic policies are essential. In order to lessen economic disparity, the chapter promotes progressive taxation, a decent wage, and tighter labor laws. It also covers the significance of paid family leave, access to high-quality daycare, and affordable housing in promoting everyone's financial security.

The chapter places a strong emphasis on the advocacy groups and grassroots movements that advance social justice. In addition to highlighting the efforts of groups like Women's March, ACLU, and Black Lives Matter, it offers helpful advice on how to get started in social justice action.

This chapter seeks to build an inclusive and fair society by tackling fundamental injustices and advancing social justice. It exhorts readers to back social justice campaigns, push for legislative adjustments, and take up the cause of addressing inequality in their neighborhoods.

CHAPTER 9: Supporting Economic Fairness
- Bridging the Wealth Gap

Democracy is seriously threatened by economic disparity because it concentrates power in the hands of a small number of people while marginalizing the majority. This chapter looks at the origins and effects of economic inequality, including tax laws that benefit the affluent and wage stagnation, and it suggests extensive changes to close the wealth gap.

The impact of economic disparity on democracy is the first topic covered in this chapter. It illustrates how a concentration of wealth may worsen social cohesiveness, lower social mobility, and corrupt politics. The economic and social repercussions of inequality are also examined, including elevated rates of crime, decreased access to healthcare and education, and increasing poverty.

A variety of policy proposals are presented in this chapter to solve economic inequality. It supports progressive taxation, which raises taxes on corporations and the wealthy and closes tax breaks that favor the wealthiest. The significance of increasing the minimum wage and bolstering labor rights, such the ability to form a union and engage in collective bargaining, are also covered.

The necessity of comprehensive social safety nets—which should include access to high-quality education, affordable housing, and universal healthcare—is emphasized throughout the chapter. It talks on how enhancing economic security and lowering inequality can be achieved by implementing programs like paid family leave, universal basic income, and reasonably priced childcare.

The chapter also looks at how financial regulation helps to advance
economic justice. It promotes more regulation of the financial sector,
including measures to stop predatory lending and safeguard customers.
Additionally, it talks about how critical it is to advance fair trade laws and
lessen corporate power in politics.

In order to close the wealth gap and build a more just society, this chapter
presents a thorough plan for advancing economic justice. It exhorts readers
to back projects for economic justice, push for legislative modifications, and
engage in grassroots efforts to advance economic justice in their
neighborhoods.

Conclusion: The Power of Unity - A Call to Action for All Americans

By the time we get to the end of "Democracy or Else: How to Save America in 10 Easy Ways," it should be clear that there are many different and complex issues threatening American democracy. But this book's message is very clear: these difficulties are surmountable. We can preserve and strengthen our democracy by working together, participating in informed ways, and remaining steadfast in our dedication to democratic values.

The Linkages Among Democratic Reforms

We have examined eleven crucial areas in this book where action is required to preserve and advance American democracy. Each chapter has offered a change-oriented road map, including topics like defending voting rights, changing campaign finance, encouraging civic engagement, and dispelling false information. These tactics are not stand-alone actions, but rather a series of linked changes that together provide a thorough plan for democratic regeneration.

Each citizen's right to vote guarantees them an equal voice in the political process, making voting rights the cornerstone of any democracy. In order to limit the excessive influence of money in politics and guarantee that elected officials answer to their voters rather than wealthy donors, campaign finance reform is needed. Restoring confidence in the integrity of our elections and ensuring that every vote counts require a complete overhaul of the voting system.

Encouraging civic participation is essential to developing knowledgeable and involved citizens. Reviving civic education equips people with the knowledge and abilities necessary to actively engage in democratic processes. Promoting public engagement guarantees that a range of viewpoints are heard and taken into account during the decision-making process, from demonstrations to policy advocacy. To hold those in positions of authority accountable and give the public the knowledge they need to make wise decisions, local journalism must be strengthened.

Creating a society that is more inclusive is essential to fulfilling democracy's promise. Fighting false information is crucial to upholding the truth and encouraging an informed electorate. Encouraging social justice tackles structural injustices that threaten the credibility of democratic establishments. Encouraging economic justice is essential to closing the wealth gap and guaranteeing that every person has the chance to prosper.

The Strength of Cohesion

The strength of oneness is the main idea that permeates this work. It is crucial for the country to unite during this period of extreme polarization and conflict. Diversity of opinion and free interchange of ideas are essential to democracy, but it also needs a common commitment to guiding ideals and principles.

Uniformity does not equate to unity. It entails coming to an understanding and cooperating to accomplish common objectives. It entails realizing that, in spite of our differences, we are all destined for the same place. The resilience of American democracy resides in its capacity to change, grow, and overcome obstacles by working together.

The Significance of Collective Action and Leadership

Navigating the intricacies of democratic governance requires effective leadership. True transformation, however, necessitates grassroots collaboration in addition to top-down leadership. There are countless instances throughout history of regular people using their commitment and action to propel major democratic gains.

These movements—which have included the fight for women's suffrage, environmental advocacy, and marriage equality—have demonstrated that extraordinary things can happen when people band together with a common goal. A powerful force for advancement and a deterrent to those who would subvert democratic ideals is the strength of unanimity and group effort.

A Request for All Americans to Take Action

We send forth a call to action for all Americans as we wrap out this book. Democracy is a participatory undertaking that demands the dedication and engagement of every person; it is not a spectator sport. The vitality of our democracy hinges on our readiness to take a stand, express our opinions, and act.

We all have a part to play in this crucial occasion. Every effort matters, whether it is defending voting rights through volunteerism, promoting campaign finance reform, engaging in local politics, assisting independent media, or addressing structural injustices. All of us need to take on the role of proactive guardians of our democracy, committed to upholding and enhancing its guiding ideals.

There is no one group or philosophy that this call to action is exclusive to. It is an appeal to everyone who thinks that a government run by, for, and with the people will fulfill its promise. It is an appeal to put aside party differences and cooperate for the benefit of everybody. It is an appeal to embrace the strength of cooperation and group effort in creating a better future for everybody.

The Prospects for a Resurgent Democracy

Although we face enormous obstacles, we also possess the ability to bounce back and rebuild ourselves. The narrative of American democracy is one of unceasing development, triumphing against adversity, and growing stronger. We may write the next chapter in this story by adopting the tactics discussed in this book and making a commitment to the ideas of cooperation and group effort.

We have the power to build a democracy that is more sensitive to the interests and goals of all of its people, more equal, and more inclusive. We can create a society in which every person has the chance to prosper, every voice is heard, and every vote is tallied. We have the ability to fulfill the potential of democracy and leave a strong and just legacy for the coming generations.

Going Forward Collaboratively

As we proceed, let us not forget that the people are the source of democracy's power. Every individual possesses the capacity to create an impact and support the group endeavor to preserve and fortify our democratic system. Let us implement the techniques and teachings presented in this book both within and outside of our communities.
It is time to take action. The urgency of this time demands audacity, bravery, and a steadfast dedication to democratic ideals. Let's take advantage of this chance to unite, collaborate, and create a more promising and democratic future for everybody.

Let us take up the mantle of democracy and carry it on with hope and resolve in the spirit of unanimity and group effort. By working together, we can make sure that democracy lives up to its promise and that the US continues to be a shining example of opportunity, fairness, and freedom for future generations.

NOTE

NOTE

NOTE

NOTE

www.ingramcontent.com/pod-product-compliance
Lightning Source LLC
Chambersburg PA
CBHW080052270726
48653CB00045B/3929